Speaker's Corner Books

is a provocative new series designed to stimulate, educate, and foster discussion on significant public policy topics. Written by experts in a variety of fields, these brief and engaging books should be read by anyone interested in the trends and issues that shape our society.

More thought-provoking titles
in the Speaker's Corner series

God and Caesar in America:
An Essay on Religion and Politics
  Gary Hart

The Enduring Wilderness:
Protecting Our Natural Heritage through the Wilderness Act
  Doug Scott

Parting Shots from My Brittle Bow:
Reflections on American Politics and Life
  Eugene J. McCarthy

The Brave New World of Health Care
  Richard D. Lamm

Two Wands, One Nation:
An Essay on Race and Community in America
  Richard D. Lamm

For more information visit our Web site,
  www.fulcrumbooks.com

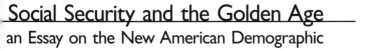

Social Security and the Golden Age

an Essay on the New American Demographic

Social Security and the Golden Age
an Essay on the New American Demographic

George McGovern

Former Senator and Presidential Candidate

Fulcrum Publishing

Golden, Colorado

Library of Congress Cataloging-in-Publication Data
McGovern, George S. (George Stanley), 1922-
  Social security and the golden age : an essay on the new
American demographic / by George McGovern.
     p. cm.
  ISBN 1-55591-589-2 (pbk. : alk. paper) 1. Social securi-
ty--United States. 2. Privatization--United States. 3.
Retirement income--Government policy--United States. I.
Title.
  HD7125.M255 2005
  368.4'300973--dc22

                              2005027907

ISBN10 1-55591-589-2 ISBN13 978-155591-589-6
Printed in the United States of America
0 9 8 7 6 5 4 3 2 1

Editorial: Sam Scinta, Faith Marcovecchio
Design and cover image: Jack Lenzo

Fulcrum Publishing
16100 Table Mountain Parkway, Suite 300
Golden, Colorado 80403
(800) 992-2908 • (303) 277-1623
www.fulcrumbooks.com

Contents

Acknowledgments

I wish to acknowledge my debt to Professor Max J. Skidmore, Department of Political Science, University of Missouri, Kansas City. He combines a thorough knowledge of Social Security with a deeply rooted social conscience. Professor Debora Dragseth of the Department of Business at Dickenson State University, North Dakota, shared her insights and experience with the emerging "Y Generation." Professor Rainey Duke of the English Department at Marshall University improved my literary form, as she generously has with some of my previous literary efforts. As always, my wife, Eleanor, gave me the benefit of her critical skill as to the substance of this book.

—George McGovern

Preface

I'm writing this book partly because of who I am—still a young guy—only eighty-three. I'm hoping to reach 100 because it will take at least another seventeen years to accomplish the things I want to do. Most urgently, before reaching 100 years, as the UN's global ambassador on hunger I want to see a good, nutritious lunch every day for every hungry schoolchild in the world. This should be supplemented by nutritious packages for low-income pregnant and nursing mothers and their infants through the age of five. Of course, it would help mightily if I could remain healthy and reasonably secure during the next seventeen years in order to accomplish these goals. I want to die young as late in life as possible. Indeed, I hope all my fellow oldsters will die young as late in life as possible. I borrow that inspired phrase from the late Dr. Ernst Wynder, a treasured physician friend of New York City who was filled with enthusiasm, imagination, and creativity every day he walked this earth.

I've had a great and lucky life, which is a good reason for wanting to extend it. Some additional years would be desirable, in part because I've picked up a little experience and wisdom along the way that might be a valuable resource in this now troubled land that we all love.

I learned a lot about life growing up in Mitchell, South Dakota, during the Great Depression of the 1920s and 1930s. Among other jobs I had as a teenager was delivering newspapers and taking care of lawns, hedges, and gardens for a cluster of Mitchell's elderly widows. These young (old in years) ladies who had survived their husbands' deaths and were living alone taught me a number of things: a respect for the elderly; a love of flowers, trees, green grass, and foliage; and pride in my work, encouraged by the praise of women, whom I've long regarded as the stronger sex. I learned also that old age—even living alone—isn't so bad if you have a measure of economic and social security plus good mental and physical health.

Beyond this, I became a high school championship debater, devoured books at the local Carnegie library, and loved the study of history and literature. I was a combat bomber pilot in the Second World War, completing a full tour of thirty-five missions and winning the Distinguished Flying Cross. I believed in the American cause in that war then. I still do a half century later—although I haven't been enthusiastic about any of the wars we've been in more recently; this includes the half century of cold war with one of our World War II allies, Russia, an enormously overdone enterprise that greatly damaged both Russia and the United States. It is said that we won that costly struggle that held the world at the precipice of nuclear annihilation for fifty years. If the collapse of the Soviet Union under the pressure of cold-war spending meant that we won, so be it.

On a brighter note, at the end of World War II our government offered the soldiers, sailors, marines, and airmen the opportunity to go to any college of their choice, all expenses paid plus a modest salary to cover living expenses. I chose Northwestern in Chicago and went all the way to a Ph.D. in history. I then went back to my undergraduate alma mater, Dakota Wesleyan, and taught history for several years. There is no way I can fully describe the enrichment—intellectual, social, and spiritual—that Dakota Wesleyan and Northwestern provided. For good measure, I had a most productive year at Garrett Biblical Seminary.

After the teaching years I entered South Dakota politics, first leading the rebuilding of the Democratic Party to make South Dakota a two-party state, then serving four years in the U.S. House of Representatives, two years as President Kennedy's Food for Peace director, eighteen years as a U.S. senator, interrupted in 1972 by my run for the presidential nomination in competition with sixteen other Democratic contenders before I won the nomination. I was then defeated by the incumbent president, Richard Nixon, who in turn was forced to resign his office in disgrace when the Watergate scandals broke shortly after the election.

After leaving the Senate in 1981—not entirely a voluntary departure—I lectured widely on university campuses across the country and around the world, an experience that taught me much about the concerns and insights of the young and their professors. For six years I served as president of the Middle East Policy Council in Washington and then four years as U.S. ambassador in Rome to the UN Agencies on Food and Agriculture.

I do not say this boastfully, but in gratitude that every year of my life has been a valuable learning experience, including the defeats and times of sadness, most notably the death to alcoholism of one of my four precious daughters, Terry. My only son, Steve, has suffered from the same addiction, perhaps America's most serious health problem, but he is now in recovery, thank God. There is no doubt that I'm a far wiser and more experienced man than in my younger days. So are my fellow senior citizens. Unless we are in the grip of some limiting illness, we are more valuable to the nation than ever before.

Thus, I write this book, partly because I want America's growing population of seniors to be appreciated for the great asset they are in experience and wisdom. I disagree with those commentators who argue that the expanding longevity of Americans is a national liability, a threat to the fiscal and economic health of the nation.

Because of my deep and growing appreciation of one of America's most important achievements of the past century, the dramatic increase in the longevity for our citizens, I want to make certain that seniors have the wherewithal and security to enjoy their older years and to share their virtues with the rest of us. An important foundation stone of those later years is the preservation and improvement of Social Security, which I will outline in this volume. We also need to fortify other sources of income, including pensions for seniors.

I flatly deny the contention of President Bush that Social Security is caught in a funding crisis that will deprive later generations of their earned retirement income. There simply is no funding crisis in Social Security, though it is possible that forty or fifty years from now we may need to make a minor adjustment in the withholding tax to replenish the Social Security Trust Fund as we did in 1983.

But do not let the president or any other critic of Social Security convince you that the Social Security Trust Fund is so crisis-ridden that today's young people will be denied their retirement income. This is nonsense. No American will ever be denied his or her Social Security benefits.

In addition to my concern for seniors, I am fortunate to have had a lifetime working association with young people as a student, professor, politician, and as a father of five and a grandfather of twelve. I suggest in the later pages of this book that there can be a natural partnership of young and old in America. Today's senior citizens are the largest of any older generation in our history. Likewise, today's oncoming youth generation is the largest in our history. As we shall see, these two gigantic groups have interests in common that could enable them to become a great power for good in our society.

I added the writing of this little book to an already busy schedule because I believe that the older years in our lives should be among the best years. We live at a time when youth is given top billing. Our movies, popular music, recreation, face-lifts, body tucks, bare midriffs, expanded or reduced breasts all cater to the premium we give to the vigor of youth.

But while we seek to prolong youth, it is also wise for a society to not only prolong our senior citizens, but to do so in a way that gives them the economic security that enables them to reach out for what the University of Chicago's Nobel Prize–winning economist Professor Robert Fogel calls "spiritual wealth." This means more time for intellectual and spiritual development. More opportunity for political participation. More reading, music, drama, travel, and recreation. More time to create their own golden age.

Introduction

"It ain't what people don't know that's so dangerous," Will Rogers once famously remarked, "it's what people know—that just ain't so." The administration of the younger Bush does its best to see that people "don't know" many things. About Social Security, though, Bush and those in his administration work hard to see that people *do* know things. Unfortunately, they are things that "just ain't so."

For the first time since President Franklin D. Roosevelt signed the Social Security Act in 1935, America has a president who is using the power of the bully pulpit to serve those who are dedicated to destroying Social Security (although in language reminiscent of Vietnam he speaks

> For the first time since President Franklin D. Roosevelt signed the Social Security Act in 1935, America has a president who is using the power of the bully pulpit to serve those who are dedicated to destroying Social Security.

of "saving" the system). Precisely why Bush is obsessed with privatization, or "personal accounts," we cannot know, but we can clearly see that his arguments make no sense. They make Americans nervous—even many Republicans—as well they should.

Bush says, for example, that the system will have to borrow huge amounts sometime in the distant future. To prevent that, he insists, inexplicably, we need to borrow huge amounts right now. He says the trust funds will be unable to pay full benefits in 2041. Therefore, he says, as soon as possible we must divert money away from the trust funds into personal accounts. Bush says the system is in crisis and will be unable to provide assistance to future retirees. The truth is that Social Security is the most solvent and dependable part of the government. Yet, because of the tax cuts he pressed for that primarily benefit the wealthy, every other part of the federal government is running at a deficit *except* for Social Security.

> The truth is that Social Security is the most solvent and dependable part of the government.

Social Security is a true success story. The system operates with unparalleled efficiency, returning more than 99 cents in benefits for every dollar that it takes in. Its administrative costs are far lower than those in any private program, or in any other government program. The trust fund contains not billions of dollars, but trillions, and is still growing. There is no funding crisis here.

Even its opponents admit that Social Security will be generating huge surpluses for many years to come. Despite this, Bush tries to frighten the American people by saying that the "crisis" is with Social Security, not with the enormous shortfalls that are here and now in the rest of his budget, deficits that are building up an astronomical national debt.

There may be a shortage in the trust fund at some distant future date, but not of the magnitude Bush claims and that his potentially dangerous policies therefore seek to remedy. Any funding problems that Social Security might at some future point really have are trivial, can be easily remedied (I provide a plan to do just this), and pale into insignificance compared to the horrendous financial crisis our president and his associates are creating in our government as a whole. If there is a flaw in Social Security, it is one the president does not address: the regressive nature of the withholding tax. I will shortly suggest a simple reform that can correct this deficiency.

During long years in the Congress and as the presidential nominee of my party, I learned that nearly all successful government programs, or for that matter private industry programs, require a little fine tuning from time to time. So it is with Social Security. But there is no crisis here and there won't be at any future time. No American Congress will ever permit this essential part of our lives to go on the rocks. Congress members are not eager to commit political suicide.

Since 1972, I have been a little more cautious in pressing bold new initiatives, than I was in winning the Democratic presidential nomination. I would not have won that nomination without doing a better job than my sixteen rivals of spelling out a positive agenda for the nation. But the conventional view, even today, is that once nominated, my views were too liberal for the American electorate as a whole. I don't buy this line, but it has been the battle cry of my critics since 1972. So let me divert from the central focus of this book for a moment to discuss the political landscape of that time that led to this characterization.

In my view, it was not my views in 1972 that were too liberal, but what my political critics said were my views. Because of my opposition to the American war in Vietnam, I was accused of being weak on national defense, although I had the most impressive war record of any candidate in 1972 or since. I was falsely hammered as "the candidate of the three As: acid, amnesty, and abortion." Why? Because I recommended that a first-time possession of marijuana be treated as a misdemeanor rather than a felony. This had the practical merit of preventing our prisons from being filled up with teenagers. On amnesty, I opposed granting amnesty so long as the war continued, but I promised once the war ended to grant amnesty both for those who planned the war and for those who opposed it and refused to participate. On abortion, I recommended the decision be left up to the states.

Is there anything radical or superliberal in any of these positions?

I make this defense of my 1972 campaign because my statistical showing against President Nixon was discouraging, and that result has created a whole industry of political strategists contending from that day to this, "Don't be a far-out liberal like McGovern or you'll lose big." I answer that my ideas were not far out or extreme in any way. If my position had not been so distorted by unethical campaign strategists, aided by President Nixon's war chest of $300 million, no one would have regarded me as an extremist.

I don't want readers to close their minds to my proposals because they have read elsewhere that I'm too extreme. I wasn't an extremist in 1972 and I'm not now. My ideas in 1972 were based on common sense and historical perspective. The same is true today.

The Real Status of Social Security

Many citizens assume that Social Security faces long-term troubles. Politicians and journalists—including those who write editorials of our major newspapers, such as *The Washington Post*—reinforce these assumptions by scoffing at anyone who questions the conventional wisdom. That conventional wisdom, though, has arisen because of several decades of lavishly financed propaganda designed to undermine the people's faith in Social Security. This is not an unfounded allegation of conspiracy. Several scholars and journalists have documented this propaganda campaign in the past, and now new and comprehensive verification may be found in a recent book, *The Plot Against Social Security* by Michael Hiltzik, business columnist for the *Los Angeles Times*.

No voice critical of Social Security was raised so forcefully over so long a time as that of the late Ronald Reagan prior to and during his first months as president. Nor was any critic more off base in his charges against the program. Reagan was doubtless sincere in his opposition to the New Deal programs of President Franklin Roosevelt, especially Social Security. But a review of his widely circulated indictments of the program over a quarter of a century make clear that he had no understanding of how well the system has served the American people.

Most Republicans as well as nearly all Democrats and independents had long ago accepted the major New Deal measures—especially Social Security.

Social Security not only makes payments to the elderly after age sixty-five; it provides income to the marital mate and the minor children if a participant dies. It also provides disability income if a participant is disabled.

The program has always been self-financing from contributions by both workers and employers. It is now the most solvent part of the government, running as usual a robust surplus in the trust fund. Virtually every other part of the government is now operating on borrowed money, including everything from the Pentagon to the CIA to the Department of Homeland Security. Some of these agencies are borrowing from the Social Security Trust Fund.

> The much-appreciated benefits of the program to many millions of Americans who have worked hard and paid their own way into retirement plus the self-financing formula have made Social Security the most effective and most popular of all government programs.

The much-appreciated benefits of the program to many millions of Americans who have worked hard and paid their own way into retirement plus the self-financing formula have made Social Security the most effective and most popular of all government programs.

Presidents supporting the program since the death of its founder, President Roosevelt, include a succession of Democrats and Republicans, liberals and conservatives—Truman, Eisenhower, Kennedy, Johnson, Nixon, Ford, Carter, Reagan (after his opening months), the senior Bush, and Clinton—who agreed on preserving and even expanding FDR's legacy.

Johnson, embarrassed by the high percentage of the federal budget going to the military—especially during the Vietnam War—took steps to have the Social Security system included in the federal budget, even though it was financed both then and since by withholding taxes paid by workers and their employers. By adding Social Security to the federal budget Johnson achieved two political gains: he made the military costs a smaller percentage of the total budget, and he could use the Social Security Trust Fund to make the national debt seem smaller. There was, however, no doubt about the support for Social Security by Johnson and all other presidents until President Reagan and the junior Bush.

Professor Max Skidmore in his excellent book *Medicare and the American Rhetoric of Reconciliation*, published in 1970, noted at that time, "It seems indisputable that Americans generally have favored the programs of the Social Security Act since its adoption ... the evidence indicates that the American people strongly supported the system since its beginning. The program seems to have become a feature of the American way of life ... the public acceptance of Social Security seems so great that opposition tends to be covert ... "

That was the prevailing view in 1970. I had been in the U.S. Senate for eight years when Professor Skidmore's book was published. I never knew a single senator who was opposed to Social Security, either overtly or covertly. Support for Social Security was as universal in the Senate as support for the Bill of Rights. During twenty-two years in the House and the Senate, I cannot recall any member of the U.S. Congress ever attacking Social Security.

One public figure who did attack the program and, indeed, the entire New Deal was a retired actor named Ronald Reagan. In his younger years Reagan had been a liberal Democrat and a labor union official serving as president of the Screen Actors Guild. But by 1954, his views had swung far to the right. He signed on with the General Electric Corporation and, in addition to hosting the company's "G.E. Theater" television program, he began speaking at hundreds of conventions, banquets, and other forums across the nation.

Early on he developed what he called "The Speech." With only slight modifications, such as mentioning some aspect of the locality where he was speaking, he gave essentially the same speech countless times over the years. He became popular, stressing such matters as the dangers of communism and the dangers of government centralism through such programs as Social Security and "socialized medicine."

By 1964, Reagan was perceived as being on the extreme right wing of the Republican Party. That year he delivered a television address on behalf of GOP presidential nominee Senator Barry Goldwater that made him a close second to Goldwater as a hero of the far right. The Arizona senator, who became more liberal in his views after retiring from politics, was crushed by incumbent President Lyndon Johnson in 1964, but Reagan went on to become the governor of California, run unsuccessfully for the Republican presidential nomination in 1976, and then, in 1980, gained both the nomination and the White House.

During nearly all these years, Reagan openly assailed Social Security and the Medicare program. As early as 1957, he asserted falsely that "recipients of Social Security today will collect $65 billion more than they paid in. And what of our sons," he cried, "the young men joining the workforce in the next few years? If he could have his Social Security tax to invest in private insurance, it would provide for almost double the benefits provided by Social Security."

Although such statements display an almost unbelievable misunderstanding of Social Security, Mr. Reagan increased his passion against the program. In 1972, he told the National Association of Manufacturers in New York, "Take for example the biggest sacred cow in all of the United States: Social Security. I have to say that if you couldn't come up with a better idea than that, you wouldn't still be in business."

In a series of three radio broadcasts in 1975, he

described Social Security as "a sure loser" and "a cruel joke." He proposed that instead of building up the Social Security Trust Fund, workers should invest in private accounts.

As he neared election to the White House and in his opening year as president, Reagan shifted his attack on Social Security to the claim that the program was in crisis and nearing bankruptcy. This, of course, was an imaginary fear. But Reagan and other enemies of Social Security convinced many young Americans that by the time they retired there would be no funds left to aid their retirement.

Ronnie Duggar, the famed Texas reporter, noted in the opening year of the Reagan administration, "In the Republican-controlled Senate, as the subcommittee on Social Security opened its hearings that first summer of the Reagan administration, an aide to the panel's chairman (Senator William Armstrong, R-CO), told *The Wall Street Journal* about a deliberate plan to fill the air with the word 'crisis.' 'It will be well-orchestrated—lots of horror stories,' the aide said." But as Duggar documented, "There was no crisis; the whole outcry would have been ludicrous if (the) facts had been made clear. Instead of following the facts, Reagan deliberately created the panic." Duggar reasoned, "One is impelled to conclude that he is using his presidency to undermine Social Security with specious alarms and arguments that conceal his ideological purpose."

Reagan strategists tried to create an atmosphere for cuts in the domestic social programs, including

Social Security, by deliberately running up the federal deficit to an unheard-of level. They did this by radically increasing military spending while drastically reducing taxes. The theory was that with an unprecedented deficit, Congress would be unable to strengthen any domestic program with additional funds.

There can be no doubt that the claims led by Reagan for so many years convinced millions of young people that Social Security would run out of money long before they reached age sixty-five. This false impression is still on the loose across the land.

Nonetheless, when President Reagan presented his proposed slash of Social Security four months into his presidency, it was soundly rebuffed, the Republican-controlled Senate turning it down ninety-six to zero. Reagan tried a second time to reduce the program by endorsing an agenda of cuts proposed by a group of Republican senators, but this too was soundly rejected by Congress.

Reagan then withdrew from the Social Security battlefield, realizing he did not even have the support of the Republican-controlled U.S. Senate. He did succeed in getting Congress to repeal college benefits for the children of deceased workers—a move that is a hardship for low-income families that have lost the head of the household.

Reagan then created a Social Security task force headed by Alan Greenspan that also included Republican Senator Bob Dole and Democratic Senator Pat Moynihan. The group recommended a modest increase in Social Security taxes that Congress accepted, and the program's trust fund promptly began climbing to trillions of dollars, where it remains to the present day—still growing. In the end President Reagan—for many years one of the most relentless foes of Social Security and Medicare—became a supporter of both. As the federal deficit continued to climb, Congress demanded a meeting with the president to discuss his budget and tax policies. Reagan agreed and then made this remarkable statement: "Everything will be on the table for discussion except Social Security. Let's leave it alone."

The legacy of Reagan for Social Security is that up to a point he was the role model for the junior President Bush. It is true that Reagan was more of a pragmatist and less of an ideologue than Bush. Pressed by the ideological neoconservatives who surround him and his constant mentor, Karl Rove, Bush is considerably more rigid and narrow than Reagan.

Reagan's pragmatism and his personal affability made many people forget that he rose to the presidency as a star of the far-right fringe of the Republican Party. In 1976, when Reagan sought unsuccessfully to wrest the GOP nomination from President Gerald Ford, ABC television asked Senator Barry Goldwater and me to be guest commentators at the two major national conventions. On the opening night of the Republican convention in Kansas City, Barbara Walters asked Senator Goldwater why, considering Reagan's support for him in 1964, he had endorsed President Ford in 1976. To this query Goldwater replied, "Ronnie is so far out in right field that he can't win a Republican nomination, and even if he did, the Democrats would beat the hell out of him."

I agreed with my Senate colleague.

Four years later Reagan was inaugurated—a prize that eluded both Goldwater and me.

It seems clear that our current president is following the pattern of Reagan. Like his role model he has cut taxes drastically—especially for the rich—while greatly increasing military spending. The result: deficits that will add trillions to the national debt, as was true of Reagan. And like Reagan, Bush has manufactured the fiction that Social Security is in a crisis and that the remedy is to encourage workers to invest in personal accounts instead of contributing to the Social Security Trust Fund. In a sense, the Bush team is telling workers, "Forget about the Social Security Trust Fund—you're on your own. Good luck in the stock market."

> [T]here is no evidence of a large crisis in Social Security now nor any reason to believe there will be in the future. This fear is based on pessimistic projections that will not come to pass unless America's economy deteriorates drastically and turns in its worst long-term performance ever.

Actually, there is no evidence of a large crisis in Social Security now or any reason to believe there will be in the future. This fear is based on pessimistic projections that will not come to pass unless America's economy deteriorates drastically and turns in its worst long-term performance ever.

The Social Security trustees write in their 2005 report that the trust fund will need some bolstering in 2041. The report for 1997 projected a different "doomsday year": 2029. It has steadily receded since then, holding at 2042 in 2004. In 1983, when the Reagan administration revised the program following recommendations of the Greenspan Commission, it was asserted that the system was in balance and would remain so with a surplus. It is reasonable to ask what happened to that surplus. The answer is that nothing happened—except an enormous increase in the trust fund, which is still growing.

Later projections became more pessimistic, not because things looked worse—in fact, they looked better—but simply because the system's trustees decided to use a different set of assumptions! The projected depletion year since then has never been nearer than thirty-two years, and it varies with almost every projection. It obviously cannot be a precise figure, since it changes constantly. No one can foretell the

> In 1983, when the Reagan administration revised the program following recommendations of the Greenspan Commission, it was asserted that the system was in balance and would remain so with a surplus. It is reasonable to ask what happened to that surplus. The answer is that nothing happened—except an enormous increase in the trust fund, which is still growing.

future with certainty.

During the Clinton administration, the country's economic forecasters were projecting deficits as far as they could see. However, it turned out they could not see very far; within a few months, Clinton's policies had eliminated the deficit and had begun to build up a large surplus. Clinton bequeathed that surplus to the younger Bush's incoming administration. Clinton had even begun to pay down the national debt, but it took the younger Bush almost no time to eliminate the surplus and to begin adding enormously to the debt.

> Social Security's enemies present the intermediate projections as though they are definite, as Bush did in his State of the Union message when he asserted flatly that the trust funds would be "gone" in 2042.

There is more. The presumed depletion year of 2041 is based on the trustee's intermediate projections, their so-called alternative II. The Congressional Budget Office projects the year of depletion to be more than a decade later. The trustees' report did include a more optimistic, low-cost projection: alternative I. That projection forecasts no future trouble, but the propagandists have carefully covered the fact that the low-cost projections even exist.

Social Security's enemies present the intermediate projections as though they are definite, as Bush did in his State of the Union message when he asserted flatly that the trust funds would be "gone" in 2042 (this was based on the 2004 projections). Journalists generally follow this line, but the actual reports do not do this. They are careful to point out that no projection, especially one over a long period, can be anything but an estimate—which is another way of saying that they are educated guesses.

Even without the trust funds, according to the pessimistic intermediate projections, Social Security's incoming revenues would be adequate to pay some three-quarters of promised benefits. Because of increasing wages, three-quarters of those promised benefits would be higher than benefits today.

Americans who read only news reports would be astonished to discover that some of the most significant statistics are favorable for Social Security's solvency. For example, about 46 percent of the population today is in the workforce. In 2030, at the height of the baby boomer retirement, the workforce will have contracted slightly to include about 44 percent of the population. That is a drop, but not a huge one. It is important to recognize, though, that in 1965, the workforce included only about 37 percent of the nation's population. Women flooding into the labor market have made a good part of the difference. In the 1960s, women worked primarily in the home. Today, large numbers work outside the home. Certainly if a workforce of 37 percent could maintain Social Security, one of 44 percent will also be able to do so.

It is this "dependency ratio"—the ratio of the active workforce to those who are too elderly, too young, or too disabled to be economically productive—that is a much more significant factor to Social Security than is the number of elderly versus young Americans. Nearly a third of Social Security's benefit checks (reflecting the "family friendly" nature of the program) go to those who are younger than retirement age, including to numerous children. The constant refrain of more retirees compared to fewer workers is a digression.

The demographic projections call for the dependency ratio never again to be as unfavorable as it was in 1965. Where, then, is the "crisis?" As economists Dean Baker and Mark Weisbrot have pointed out, the "crisis" is a phony one. The question is not one of economics; it is rather a question of politics. The people have the will to continue Social Security; the Bush administration does not. The administration would take us in the opposite direction; its policies would undermine a program that has served America well since benefits began in 1940.

> It is this "dependency ratio"—the ratio of the active workforce to those who are too elderly, too young, or too disabled to be economically productive—that is a much more significant factor to Social Security than is the number of elderly versus young Americans.

If a shortfall were to develop, it could be handled as it was in 1983. The Greenspan Commission simply proposed a modest increase in the Social Security tax, Congress and President Reagan acted, and the program again was on a sound footing. It certainly did not have to be done decades in advance, nor does it have to be done so far from any projected shortfall now, even assuming that a shortfall may someday develop, decades in the future.

Acting now to eliminate a possible shortfall in the distant future, in fact, could be dangerous and counterproductive. In 1983, for example, following the Greenspan Commission's suggestions, America began to tax its workers in excess of what was needed to pay current benefits. The purpose was to build up a huge surplus that could be drawn down to pay for the retirement of the baby boomers. It is inexcusable that after decades of higher taxes on the workers, some of Social Security's opponents now argue that paying off the bonds to accommodate the boomers would be bad social policy, because it would require high taxes on the rich.

In any case, the plan I suggest here could eliminate the possibility of a shortfall. More important, it redresses Social Security's one major flaw: the regressive nature of its funding mechanism. Before going further, let us look at the Bush proposal to privatize Social Security.

The Facts about Privatization

Bush has made the argument that private accounts, or as he now terms the same thing, "personal accounts," would provide a greater "return." For most participants, that simply is not true. There might be a few people wise enough and sufficiently disciplined to invest each payday in the stock market or some other place the money now going to Social Security. But experience tells us this is a shaky gamble. As a comparison, some people might come out ahead investing in the stock market what they now pay for car insurance or fire insurance. But who really wants to take that long shot? One of the shrewdest and most successful business leaders told me years ago that

> Social Security is a system of social insurance that protects against income loss from a variety of sources; it is not an investment scheme.

for most people, the stock market is "no safer than a crap shoot." I've found that to be true. And more than once I've been mighty grateful for car and accident insurance and for fire insurance on my house. I'm even more grateful for Social Security and Medicare. In any case, though, whether Bush is aware of it or not, considering rate of return is—like allegations of "crisis"—a *misleading* issue. Social Security is a system of social insurance that protects against income loss from a variety of sources; it is not an investment scheme.

Bush speaks of Social Security's paltry 2 percent return. Even if that were true, it would be better today than the return on many investments. But it is not true. The 2 percent figure is a phony one—no less phony (although certainly more reprehensible) coming from a president than from those who oppose social insurance because they hope to gain financially. The "return" on a given person's FICA taxes

> Social Security was never intended to make anyone rich, it was intended to help prevent people from being poor.

could be almost nothing for the person who had no dependents and died early, or it could be enormous if the beneficiary were disabled, married, with several young dependents, and had a lengthy life. No one complains about the zero "rate of return" on fire or auto insurance if one never has to collect. The purpose of such insurance is protection, not return on investment. "Return on investment" is no more appropriate as a criterion for Social Security. As a matter of fact, it cannot really even be calculated with any degree of certainty. It would be impossible to factor the value of years of protection into a "rate of return." Social Security was never intended to make anyone rich, it was intended to help prevent people from being poor. Although the system is far from perfect, it has succeeded admirably for almost seventy years in doing just that.

There are lucky ones who might do better in retirement under a private system. Most, though, undoubtedly would do worse. Some would even lose everything. The point is that private investments would guarantee that some people would fare far worse than others in comparable circumstances. Moreover, private arrangements involve risk, whereas Social Security's hallmark is stability and reliability—that is, security. Enron's former employees, for example, lost everything in their 401(k)s, yet their coverage under Social Security remains intact.

> Social Security provides a range of protections that no private arrangement can match.

Even lucky investors who might initially have a greater retirement check under a private scheme would still sacrifice much. Social Security provides a range of protections that no private arrangement can match.

Retirement checks are only part of the story. The system provides life insurance for dependents, a benefit for a nonworking or lower-paid spouse, guaranteed inflation protection, and disability coverage. Private investments provide none of these, and none can match Social Security's guarantee that however long the beneficiary lives, he or she can never outlive its benefits.

Privatized Systems in Other Countries

Some advocates contend that privatization works in other countries. On the contrary; privatizers praised the Thatcher system in Britain until *The Wall Street Journal* some years ago exposed it as a disaster. Many beneficiaries there, it reported, receive only about 20 percent of what they expected. The revelations did not inhibit the privatizers from pushing their schemes; they simply ceased to talk about Britain.

Americans know less about Chile than about Britain, so privatizers still praise the scheme the Pinochet dictatorship installed there. They do not mention that Chile's system requires heavy governmental subsidies. The Pinochet program has enormous administrative costs, often ranging upward of 20 percent, and such costs eat up a large part of any return. The system saves the government nothing, and upon occasion has performed so poorly that its return has been negative.

At the same time, it pays sharply reduced benefits to large numbers of retirees, benefits far lower than they would have received under the public system of the democracy that Pinochet overthrew, as chaotic as that system was. Chilean officials have remarked that although the privatized system has been good for the economy, it has been terrible for the citizens.

When Pinochet ran Chile and privatized its social security system, he was at the head of a military dictatorship. The one institution that had first claim on all resources was the army. It is highly significant that the army stayed out of Pinochet's system. The army remains under the public plan, and its retirees receive benefits far greater than civilians under privatization.

> It is ironic that with all his talk of spreading freedom and democracy, Bush seems drawn to a system that a brutal dictator imposed upon the Chilean people, one that has brought deprivation to many of them and has denied them an adequate retirement.

Curiously, though, Pinochet's system is the one Bush has praised as a model. It is ironic that with all his talk of spreading freedom and democracy, Bush seems drawn to a system that a brutal dictator imposed upon the Chilean people, one that has brought deprivation to many of them and has denied them an adequate retirement.

Americans should be reminded that our country also once had a fully privatized system. It failed cruelly in 1929, when the stock market and much of our banking system collapsed. The result of that failure was that millions of people had no safety net at all, and the depression was harsher, and longer, than it would have been had we had social insurance in place. That is why we have Social Security. As I have said, it makes no one rich, but it prevents many people from being poor. "Personal accounts" are just a slick way of saying, "Tough; you're on your own!"

A Plan for Enhancing Social Security

It should not be necessary to come up with a plan to counter President Bush's attempts to undercut the foundation of Social Security. Privatizing Social Security is a bad plan. The president keeps calling on the Democrats to come up with their own proposal if they do not like his—and all Democrats and many Republicans definitely do not like what he is proposing.

The Democratic answer to Mr. Bush is not a comprehensive alternative plan, nor does it need to be. Rather, Democrats are saying, "Keep hands off Social Security. Leave it alone except for a few modest improvements. We have plenty of time to work out any needed adjustments in the decades ahead. There is no Social Security crisis."

> Note that there were no demands for an alternative plan of the Republicans who killed the comprehensive health plan in the Clinton administration.

Note that there were no demands for an alternative plan of the Republicans who killed the comprehensive health plan in the Clinton administration. They faced no pressure to come up with something better. The Republican leaders and assorted special-interest groups simply set about gleefully killing any chance for all Americans to have health care coverage. Because of their actions, the country missed an opportunity to enact a reform that even many Republicans recognized was sorely needed. America is paying the price for that missed opportunity today.

It should not even be necessary to answer Bush's plan for Social Security. As the late President Johnson often said, "If something is working well, don't fix it." Commentators, though, even thoughtful ones who should know better, consistently impose higher standards on liberals, progressives, or Democrats in general than anyone has ever thought to apply to conservatives.

> As the late President Johnson often said, "If something is working well, don't fix it."

I recognize that political reality and refuse to let Bush and his associates continue to get away with saying that they have the ideas and that Democrats are merely obstructionists. After all, it is Bush and his advisers who are trying to make radical revisions and, in fact, to "disassemble" Social Security.

Countering unfair criticism of an existing plan does not mean that genuine improvements in the system should be avoided. Thus, I offer a plan not only to preserve the current Social Security system, a superb, time-tested program, but to make it even better.

My proposal will not only offer a way to remove any

My proposal will not only offer a way to remove any question about the continued viability of the trust funds, it will also make the system's funding mechanism more just.

question about the continued viability of the trust funds, it will also make the system's funding mechanism more just. I would reject benefit cuts, means tests, and increases in the retirement age—all of which are simply ways to cut benefits. We should recognize that a large majority of retirees depend upon Social Security for more than half of their income. We should thus avoid benefit cuts and take care to maintain the spirit in which FDR created America's most valuable and successful social program.

We should recognize that a large majority of retirees depend upon Social Security for more than half of their income. We should thus avoid benefit cuts and take care to maintain the spirit in which FDR created America's most valuable and successful social program.

The few changes that I suggest would dramatically help nearly all workers while at the same time boosting the economy. Note that they even would permit a far greater freedom for workers to open their own accounts, should they choose to do so, than would the Bush plan. In contrast to Bush's potentially destructive plan, they do this without the slightest damage to Social Security.

The assertion that Social Security is unsustainable

is ridiculous. The greatest shortcoming of Social Security's financing is not that the trust funds will be exhausted; it is that the FICA taxes are regressive. The worker pays the tax on the first dollar of earnings, and high-income workers pay nothing on income beyond the first $90,000. Thus, the worker at minimum wage, who needs every dollar he or she can get, pays the 6.2 percent on the full salary, while the $180,000 executive is taxed on only half, which brings the effective tax rate down to 3.1 percent of the complete salary.

The plan I present here provides a reasonable way to remedy this shortcoming. It also would eliminate any chance of an operating deficit, and would have numerous other benefits.

Proposal One, the key proposal:
Free the first $20,000 of earnings from FICA taxes on the worker, but not on the employer.
Employers would continue to pay the 6.2 percent tax on the first $20,000 of workers' wages.

Very low–income workers would not pay FICA taxes, yet would still have Social Security credits. This would reverse the current regressive taxation and would boost the economy by providing nearly every worker with an additional $1,240 to spend as he or she sees fit. A two-earner family with each partner earning $20,000 would have an additional $2,480 per year.

This could well be the broadest, most general tax reduction in history.

Workers and families could use their additional take-home pay to purchase school clothing for their children, put it toward health insurance, pay for prescription drugs and dental work, or open a savings account in the event they should be able to do so and would choose to do so. The economy would receive considerable energy from the additional amounts spent. This would be a far greater stimulus than tax cuts for the wealthy, who are not likely to spend the money immediately—and who in any case may spend money outside the country on foreign travel, luxury goods, or a resort home.

My proposal would provide the workforce with more disposable income than the Bush plan. Moreover, workers would have far more control over this additional income than under Bush's privatization plan.

Under this proposal, every person earning up to $110,000 per year would receive a tax cut, with the greatest cut on a percentage basis going to those of lowest earnings. In effect, each of these workers would have an increase in take-home pay, although to avoid having checks at the end of the year be smaller than those at the beginning, I would suggest deducting the 6.2 percent on the full salary of all workers, with the amount representing tax on the first $20,000 to be credited toward income tax. Workers could make adjustments in their withholding to raise their take-home pay throughout the year or, failing this, as it assumes both income tax sophistication and the ability to easily make changes to one's withholding status, get it back as a refund. This would avoid increasing the accounting burden upon employers and would require no adjustment for those workers who have more than one low-paying job.

This provision would help compensate for the low minimum wage in this country. It would do so with no additional tax for many of the nation's employers.

Freeing the first $20,000 from FICA taxes on the worker would, of course, reduce the income to the trust funds, but note that the reduction would be similar to that in Bush's own proposal to permit workers to divert up to $1,000 annually into private accounts. Bush has no way to compensate for the reduction except to drastically lower benefits, convert the system into a means-tested welfare program, and borrow staggering amounts. My suggestions, though, would compensate for that reduction within the existing social insurance frame-work and would do more: they would, in fact, compensate for shortfalls that the trustees pessimistically project. The precise figures will depend upon a complex variety of circumstances. They will have to be worked out, but there can be no doubt that Bush's proposal would slash the trust funds while mine would protect them. In other words, we should ensure continuation of America's most family-friendly program, not destroy it as its opponents would do.

Proposal Two:
Make the funding mechanism fully progressive by ensuring that those of upper income provide their full share to Social Security's support.

Two provisions will accomplish this:

First, eliminate the cap on the amount of earnings subject to FICA taxes. The cap is currently $90,000. This would be a very popular reform and would appeal to a majority of the American people who think that if they pay FICA tax on their full salary, others should do so as well. Higher income workers and employers with large numbers of higher income workers would have little to protest, because they already have received exceptionally large tax deductions.

There have been objections to removing the cap from those who say that paying full benefits on huge salaries could result in some benefits being too large to be acceptable in a democratic society. This could, and would, be avoided easily. As salaries rise, the percentage of lifetime income that benefits replace lowers (Social Security replaces roughly 42 percent of the average retired worker's former paycheck; for lower-income retirees, it replaces about 56 percent, and drops to around 27 percent of covered wages for those of higher income). The removal of the cap would not bring unlimited benefits; the increase would shrink to nothing at a certain point.

Another objection to eliminating the cap is that the wealthy could protest that they were receiving insufficient benefits in relation to their contributions.

All Americans should benefit from Social Security, but all should also take responsibility for supporting it. That means that the wealthy should accept responsibility along with other Americans and not pay into the system at a reduced rate. In any case, it would be well to label the additional tax as FICA only so long as it produces an increase in benefits. Beyond that point, there should be no additional FICA tax, but rather a surcharge on the income tax that would be dedicated to the trust funds. Note that this would merely be a small offset against the tax reductions that those wealthier Americans have already received in recent years.

There is precedent for removing the cap. Already there is no cap on earnings taxed for Medicare benefits. The wealthy pay far more for the same benefits than do those of lower income. They have accepted the additional tax that does not bring additional benefits.

Proposal Three:
Direct additional resources to the trust funds
to settle any lingering suspicion that they might
someday be exhausted.

If at some future date there was, for whatever reason not now visible, too large a drop in the trust fund, it could be replenished by dedicating an estate tax to the fund. Representative David Obey of Wisconsin and former commissioner of Social Security Robert M. Ball have suggested such a proposal. Others have made similar suggestions. This is sound public policy. Staunch capitalists such as Bill Gates Sr. and Warren Buffet, as well as Andrew Carnegie of the nineteenth century, have asserted correctly that estate taxes are essential to prevent the increasing concentration of fortunes in fewer hands as generations pass. This is important because neither democracy nor creativity can flourish when too few people control most of society's resources.

Such a tax would apply only to large estates—various proposals generally suggest exempting estates of up to $3.5 million or $5 million. Thus the tax would affect only the very wealthy. It would be necessary to counter misleading propaganda that it is a "death tax" or that it would damage small businesses and family farms. It would not. In any case, it would further insure the stability of future trust funds and would benefit society far beyond questions of Social Security.

Well-financed special-interest groups fiercely oppose any such tax, of course, and there would need to be clear explanation to the public of what it involves.

One such group calls itself "Americans against Unfair Family Taxation," as though it represents families and small business. This is an umbrella group for such "small" concerns as the National Beer Wholesalers Association, the U.S. Chamber of Commerce, U.S. Telecom, and the National Association of Manufacturers. It would be necessary to counter the misleading claims and advertising that will be inevitable—not the least of which would be to point out the ludicrous nature of the names that such groups choose for themselves.

Other ways for future replenishing of the trust funds, should the need ever arise, were suggested by the late Robert Eisner, Northwestern University's great economist. He proposed either increasing the interest rate the government pays on bonds that the trust funds hold or dedicating the portion of the personal income tax that is a "tax on a tax" to the funds. Currently, Social Security taxes are not deductible from federal income tax thus, in declaring one's income for tax, the taxable amount includes the amount already paid for FICA. Eisner suggested dedicating the tax on that amount to the trust funds.

An additional consideration for trust fund enhancement:

Most state and local employees are covered by Social Security, but many employees in numerous states are not. AARP, an excellent and much admired organization, supports a requirement for all new state and local governmental employees to be blanketed into the system. This has widespread support among liberals and conservatives alike. This is the last major group in society that does not have the responsibility of supporting the shared burden of financing Social Security.

In the short run, blanketing in these workers would give a considerable boost to the trust funds. In the long run, though, their retirement would cancel much of the advantage. The long-term effect thus would likely be negligible.

The American Federation of State, County, and Municipal Employees (ASFSCME) is a powerful supporter of Social Security and opponent of privatization. Nevertheless, the union has offered strong arguments against mandatory inclusion of those of their members who are not already covered. AFSCME points out that virtually all of those who are not already under Social Security are under another similar public pension system. The question may be more complex than it appears. In the abstract, these workers should come under Social Security, and no doubt ultimately will. Their arguments, though, should be considered carefully before making a final decision. That decision should not be hasty, nor is there a need for it to be. In a sense, the most compelling case for including local and state employees under Social Security is that it would treat all workers equally.

Proposal Four and Some Final Thoughts:
Devote any trust fund surplus to paying down the national debt.

The surplus should be borrowed only for that purpose, rather than being borrowed for general expenses, as is the current practice.

The economic difficulties facing the United States in years to come do not arise from Social Security, but rather from deficit spending and an enormous national debt. My proposal might appear to be "double counting," but it is not. Currently Congress and the president borrow from the trust funds and spend the money for a variety of purposes. They are obligated to redeem the bonds in the trust funds but, in addition, they owe the national debt and must pay the huge interest that the debt generates. If the trust fund surplus were to fund the national debt, it still would be necessary to repay the amounts to the trust funds, but there would be less of the national debt to pay and less interest on that debt. This would be a true "lock box."

Such a shift could involve a tax increase to maintain government programs, but that is the price to be paid for good government and for necessary services. Current policies are based on the assumption that there is a free lunch. There is not. The Bush policies, long after current office holders are gone, will bring chaos for our children and grandchildren as they are called upon to pay, not only Social Security—which will be minor—but the national debt—which will be enormous.

My plan would remove any question about the

stability of Social Security. The changes would extend to Social Security's financing the progressive nature that currently exists in its benefits structure, and they would be highly popular with the general public. Almost all workers would be affected favorably: they would be assured of Social Security's permanence and they would likely welcome adoption of the principle that the wealthy pay into the system at roughly the same rate as everyone else.

I hope the Congress will adopt this proposal or something like it. So long as ideologues are in control, it is unlikely that this will happen, but times change. The next elections may bring enough thoughtful representatives and senators of both parties to Washington to wrest control from those now in power. If so, this proposal then might make it to the president. President Bush would probably not sign it. After January 2009, though, there will be a new and perhaps a more thoughtful president. There will also be a different Congress, one that we can hope will have developed more concern for the people, replacing concern for the special interests. Then we may have a truly reformed Social Security that will continue to be America's superb system of social insurance. These reforms could be phased in over the next thirty years or so at no risk to the American people and the Social Security recipients.

Having underscored the essential strength of Social Security and a few steps that could make this valuable program even stronger and better, let us now look at the larger question of how the older years ahead of all of us can really be the "golden years" of our lives. Social Security remains one big step toward this dream, but there are other steps as well, some of which are attitudinal.

Getting Older: A National and Personal Asset

Theodore Roszak, a product of the turbulent 1960s and the author in 1968 of *The Making of a Counter Culture*, thirty years later, in 1998, wrote an important book with a new and challenging perspective, *America the Wise: The Longevity Revolution and the True Wealth of Nations.*

Historian Roszak argues that, far from being a national headache, the growing longevity of Americans and the increasing number of elderly citizens may be America's most precious asset. Far from being a nuisance for our policy makers, our families, and our society, the old heads may be a valuable resource.

Numerous writers, editors, and commentators have in recent years referred to the mounting numbers of the aging with terms such as "catastrophe," "alarming," "a fiscal train wreck," "a formula for national bankruptcy," or a "dangerous prospect."

Professor Roszak has a sharply differing view from such negative doomsday soundings. He states his thesis bluntly: "Longevity is here, it is inevitable, it is good. Our task is to stop resisting the inevitable and to embrace the good." He has concluded that the graying of

America should be a cause for national optimism and rejoicing. The older citizens, after all, carry a wealth of experience, wisdom, and understanding that can enrich, inform, and inspire younger generations. Of course, there will always be a few old fools among us just as there will be a few young fools.

If life is what each of us holds dear, then for most people extending life is a plus, not a minus. And so it is for the rest of society that stands to gain from the contributions of the older generation.

How many children and youth have had their lives enriched and warmed by loving grandparents? How many parents have found their parenting obligations made easier because of the helpful role of their own parents?

Perhaps at the age of eighty-three I am especially receptive to this line of reasoning. All of us want to believe that we are still important as the years roll by with seemingly increased momentum. Long before reading Professor Roszak's book I had rejected the notion that the growing longevity of our citizens is a national

> [T]he graying of America should be a cause for national optimism and rejoicing. The older citizens, after all, carry a wealth of experience, wisdom, and understanding that can enrich, inform, and inspire younger generations.

liability. I honestly believe that I'm a wiser man today than when I first went into Congress in 1956, at the age of thirty-four, or when I joined the Senate for eighteen years in 1962, at the age of forty.

In 1972, when I won my party's nomination for the presidency, I thought that I knew just about everything. But more than thirty years later I know that I would be a much wiser president at eighty-three than if elected in 1972, at the age of fifty. (I hasten to add that even with my lesser knowledge in 1972, the country would have been better off if I had won that year. It might even have been better for President Nixon!)

Sometimes it is profitable to listen to the advice of older heads. The late President Lyndon Johnson was one of our most successful presidents in domestic concerns including civil rights, education, Medicare, housing, and labor issues. He had an appealing vision of America as the Great Society. But in foreign policy the sure instincts that guided Johnson on the home front failed him abroad. The result was the tragically escalating American war in Vietnam—a disaster for both the Vietnamese and the Americans and a political disaster for Johnson that led him to decline reelection in 1968.

All of this could have been avoided if the president had listened to some of his older former colleagues in the Senate such as Mike Mansfield, William Fulbright, George Aiken, Albert Gore Sr., Wayne Morse, and Ernest Gruening. Such experienced military men as World War II hero General James Gavin and retired commander of the Marine Corps General Shoup would also have steered LBJ away from Vietnam. The current American invasion and occupation of Iraq—another foreign policy blunder—could have been avoided if

President George Bush had heeded the advice of older, more experienced men, including his father, the former President Bush, plus the secretary of state and the national security advisor in the first Bush administration, James Baker and General Brent Scowcroft.

Other older men in the U.S. Senate could have saved us from the quagmire in Iraq—Senators Robert Byrd, Edward Kennedy, Robert Graham, John Warner, Tom Harkin, and Pat Leahy come to mind. I strongly suspect that the commander of our forces in the first Gulf War, General Schwartzkopf, also had deep reservations about the current invasion of Iraq.

The judgments of every president are in the end his, but in almost every case it is worth hearing what the oldest and most experienced people are thinking before the final decision is reached. Needless to say, in some instances the insights of the young and those in the middle years may not only be the most original but also the most valuable. Before making such a momentous decision as committing our young people to war, a president should consult old and young, male and female, white, brown, and black, capital and labor—the whole range of American society, but especially those who

> The present generation of middle age, the offspring of the "Greatest Generation" of the depression and World War II years, will be the healthiest, best educated, wealthiest, and most productive older generation America has ever had.

have lived and learned in times both good and bad.

The present generation of middle age, the offspring of the "Greatest Generation" of the depression and World War II years, will be the healthiest, best educated, wealthiest, and most productive older generation America has ever had. This is very good news. The news is all the better in that this coming older generation will exert a powerful influence on the policies, priorities, and values of the United States.

By the year 2020—fifteen years hence—the old in America will outnumber the young. This will be good for young and old alike, and for those in the middle. Much of the true wealth of the nation is concentrated in its ever-growing older generation. These oldsters have valuable life experiences, informed cultural tastes, and political maturity.

> When I think of my fellow oldsters, the qualities that come to mind are compassion, understanding, tolerance, patience, and mercy.

In one sense our aging population represents the old dictum "survival of the fittest," but in a more important sense it is the survival of the gentlest and the wisest. When I think of my fellow oldsters, the qualities that come to mind are compassion, understanding, tolerance, patience, and mercy—sometimes with a mix of crankiness and fading memory.

Since the official senior citizen age begins at sixty-five, I've been a member in good standing for eighteen years, and it's been a good trip. In the past when the subject of aging would enter a conversation, I would say, "It's not how long you live that matters but what you do with your years."

I don't say that anymore. I want to live a long time—maybe to 100. One of the reasons is that I'll need another seventeen years to complete all the things I still want to do. Just to mention one ambition, I've written nine books, but how about an even dozen along with a batch of essays, articles, speeches, and television and radio interviews? Why quit sounding off now? Then, too, I want to see my lifelong team, the St. Louis Cardinals, win another World Series. They got to the World Series in 2004 but were swept by the Boston Red Sox. I'd also like to see the Washington Redskins win another Super Bowl. My Sioux Indian friends in South Dakota tell me that won't happen until they drop the name Redskins. The Bible tells us to love the sinner, so I continue to pray for the Redskins despite their wicked name. Beyond this, I still enjoy hunting pheasants. Once in a while I even hit one. Having reserved bragging rights, I have eyewitnesses who will confirm that on a recent hunt I got five pheasants without a miss. I remember this because it happens so seldom for me.

My generation and perhaps even more so the generation that is following us close on will achieve senior dominance. We are not only living longer, but we do so with more effectiveness and more security than preceding generations. We have the numbers and the ability to be a force in shaping life in the twenty-first century.

We know that we will be about the business of living longer than any previous generation. We also know that our numbers and our wills can make us a commanding influence in the governance of America.

"With us, history shifts its rhythm," writes Roszak. "It draws back from the frenzied pursuit of marketing novelties and technological turnover and assumes the measured pace of humane and sustainable values. We may live to see wisdom become a distinct political possibility, and compassion the reigning social ethic. Great changes, and yet they stem from nothing more remarkable than life running its full course, as it now can for so many millions more. Longevity, when it embraces so many, cannot help but be a great maker of history."

> "With us [the older generation], history shifts its rhythm," writes Roszak. "It draws back from the frenzied pursuit of marketing novelties and technological turnover and assumes the measured pace of humane and sustainable values."

William Greider, one of our most perceptive journalists, is the person who first called my attention to the increased longevity of America's aging as a great national treasure provided we and our government have the wisdom and common sense to cultivate and undergird this great resource. Writing in *The Nation* magazine of June 27, 2005, in an article that deserves a Pulitzer Prize, Mr. Greider introduces us not only to Theodore Roszak but also to Robert Fogel, the University of Chicago Nobel Prize–winning economist, and other creative thinkers who have focused their expertise on our growing senior citizen population and its capacity to enrich our society.

The Greider article opens with an array of fascinating and meaningful facts: "In 1900 Americans on average lived for only 49 years and most working people died still on the job. For those who lived long enough, the average 'retirement' age was 85. By 1935, when Social Security was enacted, life expectancy had risen to 61 years. Now it is 77 years—nearly a generation more—and still rising. Children born today have a fifty-fifty chance of living to 100. This inheritance from the last century—the great gift of longer life—surely represents one of the country's most meaningful accomplishments."

Regrettably, Mr. Greider tells us, this remarkable achievement "has been transformed into a monumental problem for contemporary politics and narrow-minded accounting."

To elaborate his point, Greider quotes an editorial from *The Washington Post*, the paper where he once worked as national affairs editor: "The nation faces a severe economic threat from the aging of its population combined with escalating health costs."

Other sources have been even more critical and fearsome, referring to our aging citizens as "greedy geezers" whose demands exploit the young and exhaust the U.S. Treasury.

One can only wonder how such critics regard their own advancing seniority. If they should make it into old age, will they continue to regard longevity as a national calamity? Do they even pause to think that from the day of our birth every one of us will spend our life getting older? Who really wants to shorten his or her life span?

One American, now in his seventies, who does not see the extension of life as either a personal or a national liability is Professor Fogel of the University of Chicago. Like historian Roszak, economist Fogel contends that America should rejoice that its citizens are living longer than ever before.

> Long ago the philosopher John Ruskin observed, "There is no wealth but life. Life, including all its powers of love, of joy, and of admiration. That country is richest which nourishes the greatest number of noble and happy human beings."

Long ago the philosopher John Ruskin observed, "There is no wealth but life. Life, including all its powers of love, of joy, and of admiration. That country is richest which nourishes the greatest number of noble and happy human beings."

As Fogel points out, Americans are now voluntarily retiring at a younger age. With the average retirement age now sixty-three, he believes that with sufficient financial security the average retirement age might soon drop to fifty-five. Large numbers of older people are looking forward to more leisure time, including the opportunity for intellectual and spiritual development, increased time for reading, recreation, and travel. Many of the elderly would relish more time with their family and friends. Considerable numbers would gain satisfaction in volunteering for neighborhood and community activities, including political, civic, social, sporting, and religious events. In times of national crisis, be it 9/11 or natural disasters such as Hurricane Katrina, many times it is the older Americans who man phone banks and help coordinate volunteer efforts, as they have the time and the ability. Other older Americans who don't want to simply take life easy after sixty-five take on different employment to follow early dreams or, as in my case, continue to speak and write at a great pace, not only achieving intellectual development, but giving back. Former colleagues of mine no longer in the Senate, such as Tom Daschle, Bob Dole, Al Simpson, Birch Bayh, John Culver, and Walter Mondale, just to name a few, continue working around the clock in a variety of public service activities. Gaylord Nelson, my closest Senate friend—a great environmentalist and the creator of Earth Day—worked in a key role for the Wilderness Society for many years after he left the Senate, until he died at the age of eighty-nine. Bob Dole was the key figure in creating the magnificent World War II memorial on the Capitol Mall—all of this after his retirement from the Senate. Tom Eagleton, after his retirement from the Senate, was a guest professor at Washington University in St. Louis (his hometown), a news column writer, a radio and TV commentator, and a leading lawyer who was instrumental in bringing the Los Angeles Rams football team to St. Louis. Another

Senate colleague, Mark Hatfield, keeps busy in retirement reading, writing, and lecturing while supporting an array of public service agencies.

There comes to mind a glittering array of other public officials who have worked diligently for long hours in the so-called retirement years—former president Jimmy Carter; famed economist Ken Galbraith; noted historian Arthur Schlesinger Jr.; feminist leader Gloria Steinem; Lady Bird Johnson; former secretary of defense Robert McNamara; former secretary of the interior Stewart Udall; Andrew Young, statesman and diplomat; Dwayne Andreas, the chief of Archer Daniels Midland; the Reverend Billy Graham; Herbert Kurz, the head of Presidential Life; Douglas Fraser, former president of the United Auto Workers; and a host of others highlighted by such giants of radio, television, and the writing press as the matchless Walter Cronkite, Mike Wallace, Larry King, Barbara Walters, Al Neuharth, the late Katherine Graham, and Mary McGrory— all working with increasing service motivation and wisdom into advanced years.

Just about all of my older friends and associates seem to want to work at some serviceable task—or many such tasks—as they grow older. They also relish their leisure hours and the time to think and read and converse with others. Such longtime friends include Robert Bernstein, the brilliant former chief of Random House who guided me into writing books, and Ambassador Henry Kimelman, who ran the finances of my 1972 presidential campaign and who has been a constant advisor over the years.

As Greider puts it, "What people want is time—more time to enjoy life and learning, to focus on the virtuous aspects of one's nature, to pursue social projects free of economic necessity, to engage their curiosity and self-knowledge, or their political values." I might add that Greider is himself a shining example of how a person can gain from each passing year. I have known him and read his words for nearly thirty-five years, since he covered my 1972 presidential campaign. He was a brilliant journalist then. But as the years and decades have moved by he has become a wiser, more perceptive man—one of our national treasures.

> "The quest for spiritual equity," writes Fogel, "turns not so much on money as on access to spiritual assets—assets that are gained privately rather than through the market or the government."

The barrier to enjoying these attractive and soul-seeking opportunities that I have described is what Fogel calls the "maldistribution of spiritual resources."

He defines spiritual resources to include a broad range of nonmaterial assets—self-esteem, thirst for knowledge, a sense of purpose, a sense of discipline, a vision of opportunity. "The quest for spiritual equity," writes Fogel, "turns not so much on money as on access to spiritual assets—assets that are gained privately rather than through the market or the government.

It is Fogel's view that "the rise of an egalitarian ethic

was one of the major factors that turned the separate American colonies into a nation and eventually led to the establishment of egalitarianism as an national creed."

Jefferson and his colleagues stated in the Declaration of Independence, "We hold these truths to be self-evident that all men are created equal. They are endowed by their Creator with certain inalienable rights. Among these are life, liberty and pursuit of happiness."

Abraham Lincoln, perhaps our greatest president, believed that the central principle that preserved the Union was the promise that "all should have an equal chance." Our founders and other great figures who have shaped the American nation did not argue that all of our citizens should have equal talent and wealth. Rather they believed that our citizens should have the opportunity to develop their varying abilities unfettered by man-made restrictions of a political, social, economic, or religious nature. The Bill of Rights spells out the personal freedoms of Americans that entitle every citizen to freedom of opportunity.

This is the freedom that has drawn untold millions of people to the United States. This is the American creed that the world most admires and that every American patriot holds dear.

The Obstacle

Unfortunately, society has not arranged itself so that these appealing opportunities are within the reach of large numbers of older citizens. Even with Social Security, pensions, and 401(k) and IRA savings, there is often insufficient income to cover the increasing length of the older years.

Many Americans who have worked hard for a lifetime—sometimes at jobs that were not very enjoyable—find themselves unable to pursue their dreams in retirement. These are the losers in old age, but so are their families, their neighborhoods, and our society as a whole.

Many older Americans must continue working long after they planned to be retired simply because they lack sufficient retirement income.

I'm one of the most fortunate senior citizens on several counts. First, in a long life I've never had a job that I didn't enjoy, whether as a teenager carrying newspapers and caring for the yards of a group of elderly widows in Mitchell, South Dakota; or teaching history as a college professor; or working for the U.S. government as a congressman, a special assistant to President Kennedy, a U.S. senator, as president of the Middle East

Policy Council, as U.S. ambassador to the UN Agencies on Food and Agriculture in Rome, and now as UN global ambassador on hunger. I suppose the word "enjoy" does not quite describe flying thirty-five missions as the pilot of a four-engine bomber against some of the most heavily defended targets in Hitler's Nazi Germany. But I believed in the American cause and received lasting satisfaction from blasting Hitler's aggressive war machine. I'm fortunate that my advanced years made me ineligible for either the Vietnam War or the current invasion of Iraq. My conscience would not have permitted me to serve in either of these ill-advised and unnecessary wars. My heart bleeds for the gallant young Americans who died in these needless conflicts. I guess that makes me "a bleeding-heart liberal."

I've been fortunate, secondly, because the U.S. government offered the G.I. Bill at the end of World War II, which enabled me—even with a wife and child—to go to Northwestern University and earn a Ph.D. in history. This excellent education and the advanced degree have opened up numerous doors to me and still does.

The government has made my "retirement" years (moving from twelve hours a day to ten) more livable with Social Security, Medicare, and a government pension covering my years in the Army Air Corps, Congress, and the federal executive and legislative branches. Beyond this, I have been able to secure enough money to be comfortable in my older years, although not rich. It would be pleasant to be even richer, but that is a low priority with me. But it's a high priority to see those who are poor in America and around the world become richer, better fed, with health care, sanitary water, and useful, rewarding employment.

Unfortunately, the picture I have just painted of my own life does not describe the lot of most Americans. I encounter people regularly who detest the work they are doing and can scarcely wait for their retirement. Even then they are uncertain of whether they can make ends meet if they leave their jobs. Many who risk retirement do not have the savings or retirement income to permit their dreams of leisure time, travel, cultural activities, and other enriching experiences. They suffer from both material inequity and spiritual inequity. As Professor Fogel puts it, "Spiritual (or nonmaterial) inequity is now as great a problem as material inequity, perhaps even greater."

In the Reagan years of the 1980s, 401(k) and IRA accounts were introduced as a replacement for the defined benefit pensions corporations and businesses had been providing for their employees. These personal accounts soon became the major form of pension security for American workers. When the current President Bush offered his pending proposals to change the Social Security system by having workers invest in personal accounts instead of the Social Security Trust Fund, he seemed to think this was a new idea. Actually, it is an application to Social Security of the 401(k) and IRA accounts pushed by the Reagan administration two decades earlier. This formula pressed by President

Reagan as a new method of pensions for working people has been a major disappointment for many Americans.

The basic threat to workers nearing retirement is not Social Security, which is safe, solvent, and sound. The danger is more real in uncertain pensions and the loss of personal savings, both of which supplement Social Security, and the always-increasing cost of health insurance.

Fewer workers are now covered by any kind of pension—a very different scenario from twenty years ago. The valuable company-defined benefit pensions that once covered more than half of American workers now reach only a third. Pensions have become less valuable, and fewer workers have them than a quarter of a century ago. In 1982, personal savings reached $480 billion and then began a long decline to $103 billion in 2004. The government now spends more money in tax subsidies to encourage the personal savings accounts for retirement—$115 billion in 2004—than Americans saved that same year.

> The basic threat to workers nearing retirement is not Social Security, which is safe, solvent, and sound. The danger is more real in uncertain pensions and the loss of personal savings, both of which supplement Social Security, and the always-increasing cost of health insurance.

All the reliable statistics point to a massive redistribution of income and wealth from the lower and middle classes to the wealthiest individuals and corporations in the last twenty-five years. That shift can only mean lower pension benefits and retirement funds for the elderly. This in turn means fewer material and spiritual benefits for older citizens—less leisure, less recreation, less travel, less time for reading and meditation and volunteer work. Instead, many oldsters continue to delay retirement as they seek income for their older years.

If the older generation is to achieve the golden years, which Messrs. Roszak and Fogel and many other believe should be our national goal, then something must be done to help older people find more economic security.

One useful step in this direction would be the Social Security improvements I have laid out in the first part of this book.

A second useful reform, long overdue, is a law that would require companies to make their pensions portable. Large numbers of workers have lost their pensions when they moved from one company to another or when the company went bankrupt or used workers' pension funds for other purposes.

With the Social Security safety net firmly in place, workers should make every effort to add security to their supplemental pension income. I believe that, toward this end, workers should insist on setting up a pension fund collectively, which they own and control so that it goes with them if their company goes bankrupt or moves to another city. Instead of relying on the handling of their pension fund by their companies, employees should be required by law to put an agreed-upon percentage into an independent pension fund directed by professional investors who work only for the benefit of the employees.

Most workers simply do not have the expertise to manage their pension (or other retirement) accounts profitably. They will do better with professionals independently managing a large group fund that spreads the risks and benefits evenly with each worker drawing his share depending on how much the worker has contributed to the group fund. Greider is doubtless right in concluding, "The employees' money will produce far more reliable accumulations if it is invested for them by professionals at a major independent pension fund that works only for them. The fundamental truth (well understood among experts) is that individualized accounts (as recommended by President Bush for Social Security recipients) can never match the investment returns of a large common fund, broadly diversified and soundly managed, because the pension fund is able to average its results over a very long time span, thirty years or more. A few wise guys might beat the casino odds, but the broad herd of small investors will always be captive to the random luck of bad timing and their own ignorance. The right wing's celebration of individual risk-taking in financial markets is like inviting sheep to the slaughter."

It is true that the sensational bull market gave those who invested wisely and, as the gambling song put it, "knew when to hold them and knew when to fold them" did well in the stock market. But that golden market is over—and probably for a long time. We may never see it equaled. But a large, well-managed fund can take a longer view of what will be safest and best for their clients rather than pursuing the bright lights of an up-and-down stock market.

A mandatory nationwide savings system in the form of the pension system I describe above would be a huge addition to the Social Security program. It would not depend on the whims of employers, it would not depend on Wall Street brokers taking a cut, as they do with individual managed accounts, and the workers' share would be portable if he or she wished to transfer to another city or another job.

Fogel suggests that such a system require savings rates as high as 15 percent of the worker's wages. Considering that Social Security requires 12.6 percent paid jointly by employers and workers, the proposed 15 percent add-on for pensions would be practical for high-income workers, but not for those at the lower end who need most of their wages for current living expenses. This could be remedied by subsidies paid to the pension fund to assist lower-income workers. By means of tax concessions or the need to attract quality workers, many employers might find it worthwhile to contribute to the pension fund of their workers. The federal government, which would monitor the pension fund against any possible abuses, might find it necessary to subsidize the pensions of lower-income workers.

Such a dependable pension system would be a

powerful incentive to workers to save more and spend less for low-priority needs.

Anyone familiar with the timid nature of most politicians in today's political climate appreciates that most of them will shy away from big ideas such as mandatory savings for all workers. The Democratic Party since the days of Thomas Jefferson and Andrew Jackson down to Woodrow Wilson and Franklin Roosevelt has been the traditional sponsor of new ideas. But in recent times the party has become fearful of thinking big to really get at the roots of the nation's problems. Forty years ago, when I was pressing for an end to the mistaken American war in Vietnam, I fell into a conversation with one of the most passionate critics of the war: my older colleague Ernest Gruening, the father of Alaskan statehood. We were trying to determine how many senators were with us in opposing the war. When I asked Ernest if he thought Senator So-and-So was with us, he said, "Yes, but feebly."

> **Anyone familiar with the timid nature of most politicians in today's political climate appreciates that most of them will shy away from big ideas such as mandatory savings for all workers.**

Too many of my fellow Democrats are "feebly" for fundamental changes to improve the lives of the American people and our brothers and sisters in other lands. Yet just about every American knows that we need comprehensive health care for every citizen with the U.S. government as the single payer. Most believe that we need to upgrade elementary and secondary education and deal with the crisis of skyrocketing costs for higher education. Most of our people doubtless know that the excesses, abuses, and profiteering of many corporate exec-

> [A] sizeable part of the American people know the 401(k) and IRA personal accounts have failed to provide adequate retirement funds while giving corporations and companies an excuse to cut back or terminate funding of defined benefit pensions.

utives require stronger government correctional measures. And surely a sizeable part of the American people know the 401(k) and IRA personal accounts have failed to provide adequate retirement funds while giving corporations and companies an excuse to cut back or terminate funding of defined benefit pensions.

The mandatory worker savings accounts with professional independent management and government monitoring are a big, new idea that, added to an improved Social Security system as described earlier in this book, will give American workers greatly improved retirement security.

A Partnership of Young and Old

I have been reading of late about the "Y Generation." This is the generation now in their teens and twenties— the high school and college-age youngsters. They both amaze and puzzle me.

But what about the oncoming Y Generation?

I want to know more about them because I have a hunch that they might be valuable partners to us old- sters. For example, they know all about cell phones, computers, e-mail, the Web, and other mysteries beyond my comprehension. With the help of my Y- Generation grandchildren, I'm struggling to master the cell phone. I've yet to complete a conversation with the wicked little gadget before it cuts off. I'm afraid I'm los- ing friends because I can't seem to remember how you get messages off the miserable thing.

Needless to say, I'm not yet fully introduced to the computer. I'm cheered, however, to encounter offices, stores, and banks that tell me their computer is "down." I confess that all computers are "down" for me.

But it encourages me that several members of the Y Generation seem eager to teach me their wondrous knowledge of the new age.

George Orwell tells us, "Each generation imagines itself to be more intelligent than the one that went before it, and wiser than the one that comes after it."

What is a generation? A generation is comprised of people whose common location in history and common life experiences lend them to a collective persona. A new generation arrives approximately every twenty years. Every generation sees the world differently. Their attitudes and expectations are influenced by what they experience in their formative years.

Here are some facts about the Y Generation:

Generation Y, born between 1982 and 2002, now in their twenties and younger, are also known as "Millennials." They are today's young Americans, many now entering the workplace. This generation exceeds 80 million, nearly twice the size of Generation X (44 million). They are considered the largest, healthiest, and most cared-for generation in history. According to the U.S. Census Bureau, Generation Y will come to represent 41 percent of the U.S. population.

Being a part of the largest generation in the world is a challenge. We will need visionary leaders who are not afraid to leave the familiar. College and high school teachers tell me that a significant portion of today's teenagers are smart, entrepreneurial, curious, creative, self-confident, goal oriented, optimistic, independent, and ready to change the world. They might become America's next "Greatest Generation." Due to the sheer size of this group, the impact of Generation Y in the next twenty years will be dramatic. In terms of Social

Security, not only will their pay-in to the system be large due to their numbers, but if early reports on their talent and drive are correct, they may also be better potential earners and thus provide more for the system.

> Generation Y is the critical mass that may emerge as a dominant force in the twenty-first century.

Generation Y is the critical mass that may emerge as a dominant force in the twenty-first century. Right now there are more teenagers alive than ever before. That might scare you, until you consider that, in recent years, a number of youth indicators are positive. During the last ten years, schools have been showing a rise in aptitude scores within every racial and ethnic group. Today's youth are graduating from high school at record rates, almost 90 percent compared to 25 percent in 1940, the year I graduated.

One might jump to the conclusion that more teenagers would mean more crime. Yet rates of youth crime, school violence, teen pregnancy, and the worst forms of substance abuse are decreasing. In addition, teen suicide rates are falling for the first time in several decades. Teenage arrests and violent crime rates are dropping at three times the declining rates of adult crime. Studies show that members of the oncoming generation believe that education is good, integrity is admirable, and that their parents are their role models. Teenagers currently form the most religious group in the United States. Their participation in spiritual activities is 28 percent, compared to 17 percent in the 1990s.

Today's teens are upbeat about the world they live in. Nine out of ten describe themselves as happy, confident, and positive. They are volunteering in their communities more than any previous generation. A recent Harris Poll found that 98 percent of Generation Y-ers are sure that they will get to where they want to be in life. Eighty-eight percent have established goals for themselves in the next five years; more than half say that they will someday work for themselves or start their own businesses. Doing work that has an impact on the world is important to 97 percent of Millennials.

They are the most ethnically diverse as well as the most affluent youthful group in U.S. history. In 1976, 85 percent of the U.S. teenage population was white. Today that figure is 67 percent, and by 2008, it will be 62 percent. (Source: *American Demographics*) The Internet has given this generation a global orientation. A recent Nickelodeon poll found that three-quarters of today's kids have friends of a different ethnic origin. One in four grew up or is growing up in a single-parent household. Three in four have working mothers. In 1993, 90 percent of fathers attended the births of their children, versus only 10 percent in 1975.

Members of Generation Y have unsurpassed technical skills; they are the first generation to have computers at home. They are multitaskers. In computer terms, multitasking is allowing a user to perform more than one computer task at a time. They pack seven and a half hours of "media time" into five hours.

They do their homework, listen to music, talk on the phone, surf the Web, and maintain multiple simultaneous conversations on a chat line.

This generation, when in charge of the remote control, flips channels. Parents complain to their kids, "Pick one channel and stick with it!" What their parents don't realize is that, as gurus of multitasking, they are watching two or more shows at once. Remember, they were raised with hundreds of television channels, computers, and video games. If they get up at night to go to the bathroom, they may stop off at their computer on the way back to check their e-mail. Their aptitude with technology has empowered them. They never experienced life without computers. Techno-savvy, they assume more "intellectual authority" in their homes and at school. How many of us have had to ask our kids for help with our computer, DVD player, or cell phone? They are team players. Generation Y has a strong sense of collaboration and willingness to work with others. They expect and accept constant change. Because they are used to the speed technology affords them, they demand immediacy.

At Dickinson State University in North Dakota, Professor Debora Dragseth reports on one student who complained to her that it took him twenty-five minutes to register for class from his apartment. In contrast, Professor Dragseth recalls her experience in registering for classes with hours in line, finally getting to the front of the line only to learn that the classes she wanted were already filled. As small children, Generation Y-ers were told that they were brilliant because they could program the VCR.

Generation Y's career choices will be driven by the quest for opportunities to play meaningful roles that help others, say authors Bruce Tulgan and Carolyn A. Martin in their book *Managing Generation Y*. An impressive number want to make a difference. According to a study by a U.S. research and consulting firm specializing in the work styles of younger workers, the top three job requests are 1.) Meaningful work that makes a difference in the world; 2.) Working with committed coworkers who share their values; and 3.) Meeting their personal goals. "They have values reminiscent of past generations. They appreciate country, family and the planet," Tulgan and Martin report. When asked what they fear most in the world of work, the most common answer is "boredom."

"The typical Millennial has a strong sense of independence and autonomy. Their unprecedented access to information gives them the power to acquire knowledge." (Source: *Growing Up Digital: The Rise of the Net Generation*, Don Tapscott)

Experts such as authors William Strauss and Neil Howe say that, "Over the new decade, the Millennial Generation will entirely recast the image of youth from the downbeat and alienated to upbeat and engaged with potentially seismic consequences for America." (Source: *Millennials Rising: The Next Generation*)

As one who has spoken to students on more than a thousand college campuses across the nation and in

Europe, Asia, and Latin America, I'm pleased to note a more liberal spirit in today's students and faculties. Many of them have a keen interest in the protection of the environment. They also support the UN and more effort to resolve international problems by methods other than war.

Businesses and others are supporting Millenials' enhanced sense of duty to their communities and the world. In a perceptive article by Brian Grow, Steve Hamm, and Louise Lee writing in the August 15, 2005, issue of *Business Week,* the authors report that major American business executives have found it wise to provide opportunities for their employees—especially the young workers—to volunteer some of their time and energy for community service activities.

Home Depot, for example, with the help of 200 employee volunteers, has built a playground with swings, slides, and a jungle gym at a local girls' school in a depressed part of Marietta, Georgia. The company, with its growing army of volunteers, is planning to build 1,000 more such kiddie parks in the next three years across the country at a cost of $25 million—all with the help of employees volunteering their own free time.

Chief Executive Robert Nardelli is so enthusiastic about the results in improved worker morale that, at his invitation, the executives from twenty-four other corporations met at Home Depot's Atlanta headquarters for a five-hour meeting to discuss the merits of worker participation in after-hours community service projects.

"More important," the *Business Week* researchers

note, "the calls for change are coming from inside the corporate walls. A new generation of employees is demanding attention to stakeholders and seeking more from their jobs than just 9 to 5 work hours and a steady paycheck. The number of Gen Y-ers … in the working world has grown 9.2% since 1999, while the number of Gen X workers remained flat, and baby boomers declined 4.3% … As a result, Home Depot and others are finding that burnishing an image as a socially responsible company helps to attract younger workers, at all levels."

Numerous other companies, including Costco, Cisco, and Albertsons, have sensed the need for cultivating social service activities to attract young new workers and sustain their morale. The point of this is that a sizeable portion of Generation Y desires to add volunteer service to others into their working lives.

Am I entirely satisfied with the youth of today? Definitely not. Too many of them seem to have scant knowledge of history and literature. They're not reading enough. Too many of them lack basic writing and speaking proficiencies. Too many lack the essentials of geography and science. These deficiencies may stem in part from underpaid and overworked teachers. Clearly America needs to improve its investment in quality teachers and students—the bedrock of our society.

Yet it is my hopeful belief that my generation of oldsters can form a useful partnership with the emerging generation of youngsters. The young may gain from the more measured pace and the experience of the old. The

> [I]t is my hopeful belief that my generation of oldsters can form a useful partnership with the emerging generation of youngsters.

old may be enriched by the optimism and enthusiasm of the young—and by their impressive grasp of the age of communication and technology. The closer I have moved into association with my grandchildren, the more I have learned from them, and from time to time, I detect ways in which I have informed them.

And there are many opportunities to do so. Grandparents are less burdened by the cares of child rearing and the pressures of jobs or the discipline of the young. Our times with children and youth are more of our own choosing, with less tension and strain than we may have experienced with our own children. Age and experience may have taught us a few things that, with a little tact and patience, we can pass along to the eager young people growing up around us.

As one who has been close to the young as a college history professor and debate coach—and in a long political career—I have been enriched by the enthusiasm, the optimism, and the idealism of youth. I'm ready to experiment with a developing partnership with Generation Y. I hope that this can become a mutually beneficial relationship that will further improve this great land we call America.

Allow me to suggest one important step that the younger Y Generation and us oldsters might accomplish in a nonpartisan political partnership. Nearly every

American knows that for many years the U.S. government has paid the medical expenses of those of us sixty-five years of age and over. With each passing year I become more grateful for this tried-and-tested single-payer system financed by our federal taxes. It has not only relieved us oldsters of the rising cost of medical and hospital care, it has relieved our families of this burden.

What I now propose is that we oldsters and youngsters form an alliance to extend this familiar, proven medical program to all Americans. We might do this in stages with a simple, one-sentence congressional action that would read, "Congress hereby extends Medicare to all Americans from birth through age six." Two years later it would be amended to read, "Congress hereby extends Medicare to all Americans age seven through twenty-one." Two years later it would say twenty-two through thirty-five, and finally age thirty-six through sixty-four. At this point all Americans would be enjoying the benefits now available only to those sixty-five and older.

Why is it logical for me to have all my medical bills paid by the taxpayer while a low-income family with several children receives no such insurance? Why should America, the globe's richest nation, be the only industrialized nation without universal health care for all its citizens? If the single payer (the U.S. government) system works so well for us old people, why wouldn't it work as well for the young, including pregnant and nursing mothers and their infants, or hardworking young parents and their children, and those of middle age?

Generation Y and my generation, if they work together as partners, would have the political power to extend Medicare to all Americans. What better way for the young and old to unite in building a happier and healthier America.

Among the many benefits of a single-payer health care system is that the government would then be able to negotiate more favorable, just prices for prescription drugs, hospital care, and medical fees. Pharmaceutical corporations, hospitals, and doctors are entitled to reasonable profits for their services. They are not entitled to unreasonable prices.

Extending Medicare to all Americans will absorb a big slice of the federal budget. But, if at long last we can learn not to repeat unnecessary and misguided wars in Vietnam, Iraq, and elsewhere, there will be ample funds for a good health care system with money to spare. To replace needless wars that kill people with a health care system that improves and saves lives is a splendid exchange. Such a commonsense trade will not only improve the lives and security of Americans, it will also elevate our now painfully diminished standing in the eyes of the world.

There are other useful goals young and old can profitably seek and attain, such as a better way to finance higher education and to strengthen our environment. We also need to strengthen and improve the United Nations—especially its peacemaking and peace-keeping capabilities. These are objectives that a youthful and elderly partnership has within its hand to achieve.

As Tom Paine put it in 1776, "We have it in our power to begin the world over again."

The Golden Age

We stand on the frontier of a golden age, one where there is no large threat to our Social Security system, one where opportunity abounds in making this system stronger for the future, one in which older Americans are no longer seen as a burden and a demographic nightmare but as one of our great assets, and one in which the oldest and youngest Americans can find not only common ground but common goals in enriching our society.

There will doubtless always be some tensions between the generations. Abraham Lincoln, speaking in a larger sense to the strain emerging between North and South, uttered these words in his first inaugural, "Though passion may have strained, it must not break our bonds of affection. The mystic chords of memory, stretching from every battle-field, and patriot grave, to every living heart and hearth-stone, all over this broad land, will yet swell the chorus of Union, when again touched, as surely they will be, by the better angels of our nature."

The "better angels of our nature" reside with a strong Social Security and a working union of young and old Americans seeking to build this golden age.